THIS IS NOT CHEESY!

Easy and Delicious Dairy-free Recipes for Kids With Allergies

by KATRINA JORGENSEN

CONSULTANT
Amy Durkan MS, RDN, CDN
Nutrition Research Manager
Mount Sinai Medical Center
New York, NY, USA

raintree
a Capstone company — publishers for children

Raintree is an imprint of Capstone Global Library Limited, a company incorporated in England and Wales having its registered office at 264 Banbury Road, Oxford, OX2 7DY – Registered company number: 6695582

www.raintree.co.uk
myorders@raintree.co.uk

Edited by Anna Butzer
Designed by Heidi Thompson
Picture research by Morgan Walters
Production by Kathy McColley

ISBN 978 1 4747 1067 1 (hardback)
20 19 18 17 16
10 9 8 7 6 5 4 3 2 1

ISBN 978 1 4747 1072 5 (paperback)
21 20 19 18 17
10 9 8 7 6 5 4 3 2 1

British Library Cataloguing in Publication Data
A full catalogue record for this book is available from the British Library.

Design Elements
Shutterstock: avian, design element, Katerina Kirilova, design element, Lena Pan, design element, Marco Govel, design element, mexrix, design element, Sabina Pittak, design element, STILLFX, design element, swatchandsoda, design element

Photography by Capstone Studio: Karon Dubke

Editor's note:
Capstone cannot ensure that any food is allergen-free. The only way to be sure a food is safe is to read all labels carefully, every time. Cross-contamination is also a risk for those with food allergies. Please phone food companies to make sure their manufacturing processes avoid cross-contamination. Also, always make sure you clean hands, surfaces and tools before cooking.

Printed in the United Kingdom.

CONTENTS

WHAT IS A FOOD ALLERGY?

Our bodies are armed with immune systems. It's the immune system's job to fight infections, viruses and invaders. Sometimes the immune system identifies a particular food as one of these invaders and attacks it. While our immune system fights, a chemical response is triggered and causes an allergic reaction. Reactions vary greatly from a mild skin irritation to having trouble breathing. Whenever you feel you are having a reaction, tell an adult immediately.

The best way to avoid having an allergic reaction is to be aware of what you are eating. Be careful not to consume that allergen. If you are not sure if that allergen is in a food, ask an adult or read the ingredients label of the food container before eating. Unfortunately, dairy might be hard to identify in an ingredient list. Have a look at www.allergyuk.org/milk-allergy/milk-allergy for a full list of hidden dairy terms.

Avoiding food allergens can be hard to do, especially when they are found in so many of our favourite foods. This cookbook will take you on a culinary journey to explore many of the dishes you've had to avoid because of a dairy allergy.

Kitchen safety

A safe kitchen is a fun kitchen! Always start your recipes with clean hands, surfaces and tools. Wash your hands and any tools you may use in future steps of a recipe, especially when handling raw meat. Make sure you have an adult nearby to help you with any task you don't feel comfortable doing, such as cutting vegetables or carrying hot pans.

ALLERGY ALERTS AND TIPS

Have other food allergies? No problem.
Have a look at the list at the end of each recipe
for substitutions for other common allergens.
Look out for other cool tips and ideas too!

CONVERSIONS

1/4 teaspoon	1.25 grams or millilitres
1/2 teaspoon	2.5 g or mL
1 teaspoon	5 g or mL
1 tablespoon	15 g or mL
10 grams	1/3 ounce
50 grams	1 3/4 oz
100 grams	3 1/2 oz
455 grams	16 oz (1 pound)
10 mL	1/3 fluid oz
50 mL	1 3/4 fl oz
100 mL	3 1/2 fl oz

Fahrenheit (°F)	Celsius (°C)
325°	160°
350°	180°
375°	190°
400°	200°
425°	220°
450°	230°

BAKED FRENCH TOAST
WITH HOMEMADE BLUEBERRY SAUCE

You've probably heard that breakfast is the most important meal of the day. But what do you do when so many breakfast foods include dairy? Perfect for a weekend breakfast, this sweet, dairy-free treat served with a warm fruit topping will taste like dessert.

Preparation time: 8 hours 10 minutes (8 hours inactive)

Cooking time: 40 minutes

Serves 4

Ingredients

240 millilitres almond milk, plain
3 eggs
1 teaspoon vanilla extract
¼ teaspoon cinnamon
¼ teaspoon nutmeg
oil, such as vegetable oil
8 slices thick-sliced sandwich bread

Blueberry sauce
150 grams blueberries
160 grams pure maple syrup
60 millilitres lemon or orange juice
½ teaspoon arrowroot powder

Tools

large mixing bowl
measuring spoons/scales
whisk
20 x 20-centimetre (8 x 8-inch)
   baking dish
foil
small saucepan

Allergen alert!

Swap rice milk for the
almond milk if you need to avoid
both dairy and tree nuts.

Trade plain sandwich bread
for wheat-free bread if
you're allergic to wheat.

Skip the eggs if you have an egg
allergy. You won't miss them!

1. Add the almond milk, eggs, vanilla, cinnamon and nutmeg to a large mixing bowl.

2. Whisk until the eggs and almond milk are mixed well. Set aside.

3. Grease the baking dish by rubbing some oil on the bottom and sides of the dish.

4. Tear the bread slices into 5-centimetre (2-inch) chunks and place in the baking dish.

5. Pour the egg/almond milk mixture over the top of the bread. It's OK if not all the bread is covered. When the bread sits in the refrigerator, it will soak up the mixture.

6. Cover the dish with foil and refrigerate overnight.

7. Preheat oven to 180°C to bake.

8. Leave foil on the dish and place in oven. Bake for 20 minutes. Remove foil carefully and bake an additional 20 minutes.

9. Make your sauce while the French toast bakes. Combine blueberries, maple syrup and juice in a small saucepan.

10. Place mixture on hob on medium-high heat until it begins to bubble.

11. Turn the heat down to medium and add the arrowroot powder.

12. Allow sauce to simmer for about five minutes and then remove from hob.

13. Spoon out a portion of the French toast bake onto a plate and top with blueberry sauce. Enjoy!

PEACHES 'N' CINNAMON OVERNIGHT PORRIDGE

Porridge is one of many breakfast foods made with milk. Fortunately, almond milk is a great substitute that steers clear of dairy. Mix the ingredients and stow away in the refrigerator the night before for a grab-and-go breakfast you don't have to cook!

Preparation time: 10 minutes

Cooking time: 8 hours (inactive)

Serves 4

Ingredients

2 peaches

200 grams rolled oats

480 millilitres almond milk

½ teaspoon cinnamon

2 tablespoons pure maple syrup

Tools

chopping board

chef's knife

mixing bowl

measuring spoons/scales/jug

mixing spoon

4 small food containers with lids

Allergen alert!

If you are allergic to both
dairy and tree nuts, switch
the almond milk for rice milk.

1. Using the knife and chopping board, slice the peaches. Place the peaches in the mixing bowl.

2. Add oats, almond milk, cinnamon and maple syrup to the bowl, and mix to combine.

3. Spoon the mixture evenly into the four containers and cover with lids.

4. Place in refrigerator overnight.

5. Enjoy for breakfast the next day!

CHEF'S TIP

Keep your chopping board from moving
by placing a damp piece of kitchen roll
underneath it. This will keep your cutting
surface sturdy and stable!

PIZZA SCRAMBLE

Pizza for breakfast? With a few twists to the ingredient list, you can forego the milk and cheese. You'll want to set your alarm clock early for this spin on a classic that's easy to make and tasty to eat!

Preparation time: 10 minutes

Cooking time: 10 minutes

Serves 4

Ingredients

4 slices sandwich bread
2 eggs
1 tablespoon water
2 teaspoons oil
60 grams pizza sauce or tomato sauce
4 tablespoons nutritional yeast

Tools

toaster
mixing bowl
whisk
non-stick frying pan
spatula
large baking tray

Allergen alert!

Wheat-free bread can take the place of normal sandwich bread in this recipe.

Switch out scrambled eggs with chopped avocado if you have an egg allergy.

1. Preheat the grill to high.

2. Toast the slices of bread in toaster until golden brown. Set aside.

3. Crack the eggs into a mixing bowl and add the water. Whisk until the yolks and whites are blended. Set aside.

4. Heat the oil on the hob on medium heat in a non-stick frying pan.

5. Add the eggs. Stir with spatula until cooked and liquid is absorbed. Remove from heat.

6. Spread the pizza or tomato sauce on the toasted bread slices.

7. Arrange the scrambled eggs evenly on top of the sauce.

8. Sprinkle tablespoon of nutritional yeast over the eggs on each piece of toast.

9. Arrange toasts on a large baking tray, and place in oven for about three minutes.

10. Remove from oven and serve hot.

CHEF'S TIP

Pump up your protein intake by adding some of your favourite allergen-free meat to your scramble!

CHICKEN AND WILD RICE
SOUP

Craving a creamy comfort food?
Some soups use milk to create
a smooth, creamy texture. Coconut
milk takes the place of dairy in this
creamy concoction. Perfect on a cool
autumn day, this chicken and wild
rice soup will warm you right up.

Preparation time: 10 minutes

Cooking time: 1 hour

Serves 4

Ingredients

1 onion

2 carrots

1 tablespoon oil

960 millilitres chicken broth

455 grams skinless, boneless chicken thighs

185 grams wild rice/brown rice mix

1 teaspoon dried thyme

240 millilitres coconut milk

salt and pepper

Tools

chopping board

chef's knife

vegetable peeler

large saucepan

measuring spoons/scales/jug

Allergen alert!

If you have a soya allergy, make sure your chicken broth is certified soya free.

Carefully check the rice mix package for your allergens. Some brands may contain wheat or soya.

1. Peel and chop the onion.

2. Peel the carrots using a vegetable peeler, then slice each carrot.

3. Add the oil, onion and carrots to a large saucepan over medium heat. Cook for about five minutes, or until the vegetables start to soften.

4. Add the chicken broth and bring to a simmer.

5. Cut the chicken thighs into 2.5-centimetre (1-inch) cubes while the broth is warming.

6. Add the chicken to the bubbling broth, and cook for 10 minutes.

7. Pour the rice mix and thyme into the saucepan and reduce the heat to medium-low. Cook for about 45 minutes, stirring occasionally.

8. Add the coconut milk and simmer for five minutes, until thickened.

9. Season the soup with salt and pepper a pinch at a time until seasoned to your liking.

10. Serve hot in bowls.

CHEF'S TIP

Cutting an onion can make your eyes tear up. To avoid irritating your peepers, pop the onion in the freezer for about 10 minutes before chopping.

RANCH CHICKEN BITES

Did you know that fried chicken is often made with buttermilk? Acids in the buttermilk break down the chicken to make it juicy and tender. But don't take chicken strips off the menu yet! The acids in yogurt work in the same way. Crispy on the outside, juicy on the inside, these chicken strips with dipping sauce are sure to please.

Preparation time: 20 minutes
Cooking time: 20 minutes
Serves 4

Ingredients

470 grams coconut milk yogurt
1 tablespoon dried parsley
2 teaspoons dried dill
1 teaspoon garlic powder
1 teaspoon onion powder
1 teaspoon lemon juice
½ teaspoon salt
½ teaspoon ground black pepper
2 boneless, skinless chicken breasts
salt and pepper
50 grams corn flakes
60 millilitres olive oil

Tools

measuring spoons/scales/jug
mixing bowls
non-wooden spoon
cling film
chopping board
chef's knife
large resealable bag
rolling pin
plate
large frying pan
spatula or tongs

Allergen alert!

If you are allergic to wheat, make sure
your corn cereal is certified wheat free.

1. Combine the coconut milk yogurt, parsley, dill, garlic powder, onion powder, lemon juice, salt and pepper in a mixing bowl. Stir well with a spoon and set aside.

2. Cut each of the chicken breasts into 4 equal strips (8 total), and sprinkle lightly with salt and pepper on both sides.

3. Separate 1 cup of the yogurt mix and place in a second mixing bowl.

4. Add chicken to one of the bowls and stir to coat.

5. Cover the other bowl of yogurt mix with cling film and place in refrigerator until later.

6. Pour the corn flakes into the resealable bag and seal. Set the bag on a counter or surface. Gently crush the cereal by tapping the bag with the rolling pin, until the cereal resembles breadcrumbs. Pour the crushed cereal onto a plate.

7. Set a large frying pan on the hob on medium heat. Add the oil.

8. Roll each piece of chicken around in the crumbs, until covered.

9. Place the chicken in the frying pan, avoiding splashes. Cook for about five minutes per side or until golden brown on the outside and no longer pink inside.

10. Remove chicken from frying pan and place on a plate lined with kitchen roll to soak up excess oil.

11. Serve hot with remaining yogurt dipping sauce.

15

CREAMY MASHED
POTATOES

Mashed potatoes get their smooth, creamy texture from butter and cream or milk. That's a lot of dairy products to avoid, but don't despair! Grab some spuds and get started on this alternative recipe that is even better than the original!

Preparation time: 10 minutes

Cooking time: 25 minutes

Serves 4

Ingredients

680 grams Yukon gold potatoes, plus water and salt for cooking

60 millilitres chicken broth

60 millilitres rice milk

3 tablespoons olive oil

½ teaspoon salt

½ teaspoon ground black pepper

Tools

vegetable peeler

chopping board

chef's knife

large saucepan

measuring spoons/scales/jug

small saucepan

colander

potato masher

Allergen alert!

If you follow a soya-free diet, check the ingredients list on the broth to make sure it is certified soya free.

1. Clean potatoes under running water and peel using a vegetable peeler.

2. Cut into 5-centimetre (2-inch) cubes and place in a large saucepan.

3. Add enough water to cover the potatoes in the pan. Add 1 tablespoon salt.

4. Place pan on hob on medium-high and bring to a boil. Once boiling, turn the heat down to simmer. Cook for 20 minutes or until tender.

5. Place the chicken broth, rice milk, olive oil, salt and pepper in a small saucepan. Cook over medium heat until it barely bubbles. Remove from heat and set aside.

6. Drain the potatoes and return them to the pan. Pour about half of the warm rice milk/broth mixture over the potatoes.

7. Use a potato masher to gently mash the potatoes. Add more liquid a little at a time until potatoes are fluffy.

8. Taste for seasoning. If they need a little more salt, add a pinch at a time.

9. Serve hot with Swedish Meatballs or alongside any of your favourite dinnertime main courses.

SWEDISH MEATBALLS

One of Scandinavia's prized dishes gets its fame for soft and tender meatballs smothered in a cream sauce. You can re-create this savoury entrée without the cream! This delicious, comforting dish tastes great on top of the Creamy mashed potatoes.

Preparation time: 30 minutes

Cooking time: 30 minutes

Serves 4

Ingredients

Meatballs

1 small onion
455 grams pork mince
1 teaspoon salt
½ teaspoon pepper
¼ teaspoon ground nutmeg
¼ teaspoon ground cardamom

Sauce

480 millilitres beef broth
120 millilitres coconut cream
2 tablespoons arrowroot powder
salt and pepper, to taste

Tools

large baking tray
baking parchment
chopping board
chef's knife
box grater
large mixing bowl
measuring spoons/scales/jug
large frying pan
whisk

Allergen alert!

If you follow a soya-free diet, check the
ingredients list on the beef broth
to make sure it is certified free of soya.

1. Preheat oven to 190°C. Line a large baking tray with baking parchment and set aside.

2. Cut the onion in half and peel the skin off using the chopping board and chef's knife. Then grate it using the side of the box grater with the smallest holes.

3. Place grated onion in the large mixing bowl and set aside.

4. Add the pork, salt, pepper, nutmeg and cardamom to the bowl.

5. Squish the mixture with your hands until everything is mixed well.

6. Use a spoon to roll meatballs. Evenly scoop out portions (about 2 tablespoons each) of the meat mixture, and roll between palms.

7. Place the meatballs on the baking tray 1.3 centimetre (½ inch) apart. Bake in the oven for about 20 minutes or until no longer pink inside.

8. Make the sauce while the meatballs bake. Combine the beef broth, coconut cream and arrowroot powder in a large frying pan. Whisk ingredients quickly to dissolve.

9. Bring mixture to a low simmer over medium heat until thickened slightly.

10. Add the meatballs to the frying pan with the sauce when they are done and stir well. Add salt and pepper a pinch at a time until seasoned to your liking.

11. Serve hot. This dish also tastes great on top of the Creamy mashed potatoes. Add a little sauce to top it off.

TACO SALAD

Head to Mexico for this dairy-free delight! Crispy and fresh, this Mexican-inspired salad avoids the cheese and sour cream but adds many tantalizing ingredients.

Preparation time: 45 minutes
(30 minutes inactive)

Cooking time: 20 minutes

Ingredients

2 boneless, skinless chicken breasts
2 tablespoons olive oil
1 tablespoon lime juice
1 tablespoon ground cumin
2 tablespoons chilli powder
1 teaspoon dried oregano
½ teaspoon salt
½ teaspoon ground black pepper
25 grams chopped romaine lettuce
2 ripe tomatoes
1 small red onion, peeled
285 grams tinned sweetcorn, drained
25 grams corn tortilla strips

Avocado dressing
2 ripe avocados
240 millilitres full-fat coconut milk
2 tablespoons lime juice
1 teaspoon dried dill
1 teaspoon garlic powder
1 teaspoon dried thyme
½ teaspoon salt
½ teaspoon ground black pepper

Tools

2 chopping boards, one for raw
    chicken and one for vegetables
chef's knife
2 large mixing bowls
measuring spoons/scales/jug
whisk
cling film
blender
large frying pan
tongs

1. Cut the pieces of chicken into 2.5-centimetre (1-inch) chunks and set aside.

2. Whisk together the oil, lime juice, cumin, chilli powder, oregano, salt and pepper in one large mixing bowl until blended.

3. Add the chicken, and stir to coat. Cover with cling film and allow chicken to marinate for 30 minutes.

4. Make the avocado cream dressing while the chicken marinates. Ask an adult to help you cut the avocados in half and remove the pits. Scoop out the pulp and place in a blender with remaining dressing ingredients.

5. Blend on high until consistency is thin, adding water 1 tablespoon at a time, if necessary.

6. Chop tomatoes and onion and set aside.

7. When the chicken is done marinating, heat a large frying pan on the hob on medium.

8. Add the chicken and marinade to the frying pan. Stir occasionally while the meat cooks, about seven minutes, or until no longer pink.

9. Assemble the salad in the second large mixing bowl. Add the lettuce, tomatoes, onion, sweetcorn and chicken. Drizzle the avocado dressing lightly over the salad and toss gently with tongs to mix. Top with the tortilla strips and serve with more avocado cream dressing, if desired.

Allergens eradicated!

No major food allergens found here!

CREAMY **PASTA** CARBONARA

Traditionally, this dish is made
with both cream and eggs. But you
won't be missing them at all with
this flavourful pasta bowl.

Preparation time: 10 minutes

Cooking time: 20 minutes

Serves 4

Ingredients

4 slices thick-sliced bacon

1 small onion

1 tablespoon olive oil

225 grams uncooked spaghetti,
  plus water and salt for cooking

365 millilitres plain rice milk

3 teaspoons arrowroot powder

1 teaspoon garlic powder

150 grams frozen peas

2 tablespoons nutritional yeast

salt and pepper

Tools

chopping board

chef's knife

large frying pan

measuring spoons/scales/jug

large saucepan

colander

whisk

tongs

Allergen alert!

If you have a wheat allergy, be aware of your bacon! Make sure the label reads certified wheat free.

You should also use wheat-free pasta if you are allergic to wheat.

1. Carefully cut the bacon into 1.3-cm (½-inch) pieces using a chopping board and chef's knife. Place bacon pieces in a large frying pan.

2. Peel and chop the onion and add to the frying pan along with the olive oil.

3. Place frying pan with bacon, onion and olive oil onto the hob on medium heat. Slowly cook until the bacon is crisp and onions tender. Look out for splashes! Remove from heat when done.

4. Ask an adult to help you drain the fat from the frying pan, and set aside.

5. Fill a large saucepan ¾ full of water and add 1 tablespoon salt. Put the pan on the hob on high heat until it begins to boil.

6. Reduce the heat and add the pasta, cooking according to package directions until done. Drain and set aside.

7. Place the frying pan with the bacon and onions back on the hob on medium-high heat.

8. Add rice milk, arrowroot powder and garlic powder to the pan. Whisk quickly to dissolve powders.

9. When the liquid starts to bubble, reduce the heat to medium and continue whisking until it thickens. Add more arrowroot powder, 1 teaspoon at a time for more thickness.

10. Add the drained pasta, frozen peas and nutritional yeast to the frying pan and toss gently with tongs. Taste sauce, and add salt and pepper as needed, a pinch at a time.

11. Serve hot with extra nutritional yeast on the side to sprinkle on top.

NO-CHEESE
VEGGIE DIP

You'd never guess this cheese sauce doesn't actually include cheese. Ooey-gooey and so delicious – it makes all vegetables taste good!

Preparation time: 15 minutes

Makes 1 serving

Ingredients

2 tablespoons dairy-free spread
1 tablespoon plain flour
180 millilitres rice milk
120 grams nutritional yeast
1 teaspoon mustard powder
1 teaspoon salt
½ teaspoon black pepper

Tools

measuring spoons/scales/jug
medium frying pan
whisk

Allergen alert!

Make sure you use a wheat-free
flour mix if you have a wheat allergy.

1. Melt the dairy-free spread in a medium-sized frying pan on medium-high heat.

2. Add the flour and whisk until the mixture resembles wet sand.

3. Pour in the milk, whisking quickly at the same time.

4. When the mixture begins to bubble, turn the heat down to medium.

5. Add the nutritional yeast, mustard powder, salt and pepper, and whisk again to combine.

6. Allow the sauce to cook for about five minutes, or until it thickens slightly. If it is too runny, add flour 1 teaspoon at a time until it thickens to your desired thickness.

7. Remove from heat and serve hot.

CHEF'S TIP

This dip can also be drizzled on top of your favourite cooked veggies. You can even stir in a few tablespoons with cooked pasta for another favourite — mac and cheese!

BANANA ICE CREAM

Ice cream is a dessert loaded with dairy. But you can still go cold and creamy with a simple banana creation. You only need two ingredients to make this imitation ice cream on a hot summer's day!

Preparation time: 2 hours and 10 minutes (2 hours inactive)

Serves 4

Ingredients

4 very ripe bananas
½ teaspoon vanilla extract

Tools

chopping board
butter knife
freezer-safe resealable bag
measuring spoons
food processor or blender

Allergens eradicated!

No major food allergens found here!

1. Peel the bananas and slice into 2.5-centimetre (1-inch) thick rounds on a chopping board.

2. Put the banana rounds into a resealable bag and place in a freezer for at least two hours.

3. Add the frozen bananas and vanilla extract to a food processor or blender. Use the pulse button to chop the bananas into chunks.

4. Set the food processor or blender on high speed. Closely watch the bananas blend until they have a consistency like soft-serve ice cream. It can take several minutes.

5. Serve immediately, or freeze in an airtight, freezer-safe container and keep for up to one week.

CHEF'S TIP

Add extras such as strawberries, raspberries, mangoes or allergen-free chocolate to your ice cream!

HOT CHOCOLATE
WITH WHIPPED CREAM

No dairy, no problem. You can still warm up on a cold winter's evening with a hot mug of this chocolatey delight!

Preparation time: 8 hours 10 minutes (8 hours inactive)

Cooking time: 5 minutes

Serves 4

Ingredients

Coconut whipped cream

240 millilitres coconut cream

60 grams icing sugar

½ teaspoon vanilla extract

Hot chocolate

950 millilitres rice milk or
   unsweetened almond milk

50 grams semi-sweet cocoa powder

175 grams pure honey

2 teaspoons vanilla extract

Tools

tin opener

medium mixing bowl

electric hand mixer with
   whisk attachment

measuring spoons/scales/jug

large saucepan

spoon

Allergen alert!

If you have a tree nut allergy, make sure
   your chocolate is certified nut free.

1. Place the coconut cream in the refrigerator overnight before whipping.

2. Add the cream to a medium-sized mixing bowl.

3. Using the electric hand mixer on high, whip the coconut cream until light and fluffy.

4. Add the icing sugar and vanilla extract. Whip on high for another 30 seconds until combined. Place finished cream in refrigerator.

5. Make the hot chocolate while the whipped cream chills. Combine all the hot chocolate ingredients in a large saucepan and stir well.

6. Place on the hob on medium heat. Slowly heat the liquid to avoid burning the chocolate. When it just begins to bubble, it's ready.

7. Pour hot chocolate into mugs and top with a dollop of coconut whipped cream.

8. Store leftover coconut cream in an airtight container in refrigerator for up to one week.

BERRY NUTRITIOUS **SMOOTHIE**

Who says you need milk to make a super thick shake? With a blender and some fruity flavours, you can turn your kitchen into a smoothie stall to make this sweet treat that's easy to make and take with you!

Preparation time: 5 minutes

Makes 1 smoothie

Ingredients

140 grams frozen mixed berries
1 banana
180 millilitres rice milk
2 tablespoons honey
½ teaspoon vanilla extract

Tools

measuring spoons/scales/jug
blender

Allergens eradicated!

No major food allergens found here!

1. Combine the frozen berries, banana, rice milk, honey and vanilla extract in the jug of a blender.

2. Pulse 5–6 times to break up the chunks, and then turn to high until smooth.

3. Serve in a glass and enjoy immediately.

CHEF'S TIP

For a super thick smoothie, add a handful of ice cubes to the blender.

GLOSSARY

assemble put all the parts of something together

blend mix together, sometimes using a blender

boil heat until large bubbles form on top of a liquid; the boiling point for water is 100°C (212°F)

concoction mixture of different things

consume eat or drink something

dissolve incorporate a solid food into a liquid by melting or stirring

drizzle let a substance fall in small drops

mash smash a soft food into a lumpy mixture

pit single central seed or stone of some fruits

pulp soft juicy or fleshy part of a fruit or vegetable

simmer keep just below boiling when cooking or heating

slice cut into thin pieces with a knife

whisk stir a mixture rapidly until it's smooth

READ MORE

Dairy-free Delicious, Katy Salter (Quadrille Publishing, 2015)

The Allergy-Free Family Cookbook, Fiona Heggie and Ellie Lux (Orion, 2015)

The Kids Only Cookbook, Sue Quinn (Quadrille Publishing, 2013)

Ultimate Children's Cookbook (Dorling Kindersley, 2010)

WEBSITE

www.allergyuk.org
If you have any allergies, this is the website to go to. It provides lots of useful information and a helpline.